HISPANIC LEADERS OF COURAGE

CESAR CHAVEZ

EZRA E. KNOPP

Published in 2026 by The Rosen Publishing Group, Inc.
2544 Clinton Street, Buffalo, NY 14224

Copyright © 2026 by The Rosen Publishing Group, Inc.

All rights reserved. No part of this book may be reproduced in any form without permission in writing from the publisher, except by a reviewer.

First Edition

Editor: Nathalie Humphrey
Book Design: Michael Flynn

Photo Credits: Cover, p. 1 Frances Roberts/Alamy Stock Photo; (series background) Sergei Mishchenko/Shutterstock.com; p. 5 https://commons.wikimedia.org/wiki/File:Cesar_Chavez_40915a_(cropped2).tif?page=1; p. 7 Tim Roberts Photography/Shutterstock.com; p. 9 courtesy of the Library of Congress; p. 11 https://commons.wikimedia.org/wiki/File:US_Navy_110512-N-DX698-001_A_photo_illustration_of_the_Military_Sealift_Command_dry_cargo_and_ammunition_ship_USNS_Cesar_Chavez_(T-AKE_14).jpg; p. 13 Official White House Photo byPete Souza; p. 15 https://commons.wikimedia.org/wiki/File:Cesar_Chavez_and_Brown_Berets_at_peace_rally.jpg; p. 17 https://commons.wikimedia.org/wiki/File:CAESAR_CHAVEZ,_MIGRANT_WORKERS_UNION_LEADER_-_NARA_-_544069.jpg; p. 19 https://commons.wikimedia.org/wiki/File:Cesar_Chavez_on_march_from_Mexican_border_to_Sacramento_with_UFW_workers.jpg; p. 21 Photo Win1/Shutterstock.com.

Library of Congress Cataloging-in-Publication Data

Names: Knopp, Ezra E., author.
Title: Cesar Chavez / Ezra E. Knopp.
Description: Buffalo, NY : PowerKids Press, [2026] | Series: Hispanic
   leaders of courage | Includes bibliographical references and index.
Identifiers: LCCN 2024044376 (print) | LCCN 2024044377 (ebook) | ISBN
   9781499451047 (library binding) | ISBN 9781499451030 (paperback) | ISBN
   9781499451054 (ebook)
Subjects: LCSH: Chavez, Cesar, 1927-1993–Juvenile literature. | Labor
   leaders–United States–Biography–Juvenile literature. | Mexican
   American migrant agricultural laborers–Biography–Juvenile literature.
   | United Farm Workers–History–Juvenile literature.
Classification: LCC HD6509.C48 K66 2026 (print) | LCC HD6509.C48 (ebook)
   | DDC 331.88/13092 [B]–dc23/eng/20241004
LC record available at https://lccn.loc.gov/2024044376
LC ebook record available at https://lccn.loc.gov/2024044377

Manufactured in China

Some of the images in this book illustrate individuals who are models. The depictions do not imply actual situations or events.

CPSIA Compliance Information: Batch #QSPK26. For Further Information contact Rosen Publishing at 1-800-237-9932.

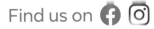

CONTENTS

Protecting Farmers 4
Yuma, Arizona 6
Moving to California 8
All Grown Up 10
Helen Fabela Chavez 12
Work Begins 14
The National Farm
 Workers Association 16
Rights for Farmers 18
A Lasting Impact 20
A Life of Leadership 21
Glossary 22
For More Information 23
Index 24

Protecting Farmers

Farmers are an important part of our community. But in the 1900s, many farmers and farmworkers weren't treated well. Cesar Chavez wanted to change that. He believed that the **civil rights** of farmers, people who work on farms, and Mexican Americans like him needed to be **protected**.

Yuma, Arizona

Chavez was born in Yuma, Arizona, on March 31, 1927. He lived and worked on farmland his family owned. When Chavez was 10, his family lost the farm during the **Great Depression**. After they lost the farm, his family moved to California looking for work.

Yuma, Arizona

Moving to California

In California, Chavez and his family worked on many different farms. Chavez saw how poorly farmers and farmworkers were treated. Workers were often not paid for their work and forced to live in bad **conditions**. They often worked long hours and didn't have clean water to drink.

All Grown Up

Chavez's parents thought school was very important. Chavez went to over 30 different schools. After he finished his education, he kept reading and taught himself a lot more. In 1946, he joined the U.S. Navy and served after World War II. He served for two years.

Helen Fabela Chavez

Chavez returned to California after he left the Navy. He then married his girlfriend, Helen Fabela. The two would have eight children together. Fabela pushed Chavez to fight for the rights of farmworkers. She also **supported** Chavez by working on farms to make money.

Work Begins

In 1952, Chavez joined the Community Service Organization (CSO). This group supported the civil rights of Latinos in America. The CSO worked to stop **discrimination** towards Latinos in their communities. It helped Latin Americans gain the right to vote and showed how voting could help Latinos gain respect.

The National Farm Workers Association

By the early 1960s, Cesar became the national director of the CSO. He stayed there for four years. He wanted to do much more though. He always wanted to protect the rights of farmworkers. In 1962, he left the CSO to start the National Farm Workers Association.

Rights for Farmers

The National Farm Workers Association fought to get better pay, better working conditions, and more respect for farmworkers. In 1965, he led his first **strike**. This strike was for people who picked grapes. The strike lasted five years, but led to better pay and protection for grape pickers.

A Lasting Impact

Chavez spent the rest of his life working to gain more rights and protection for farmworkers. Because of Chavez, many farmworkers have better pay and safer conditions to work in. Today, the National Farm Workers Association, now called United Farm Workers of America, continues the work Chavez started.

A Life of Leadership

March 31, 1927
Cesar Chavez is born in Yuma, Arizona.

1946
Chavez enters the Navy at 18.

1952
Chevez joins the Community Service Organization (CSO).

1962
Chavez leaves the CSO to start the National Farm Workers Association.

1965
Chavez leads his first strike.

April 23, 1993
Chavez dies in San Luis, Arizona, at the age of 66.

GLOSSARY

civil rights: The personal freedoms granted to U.S. citizens by law.

condition: The way things are at a time or in a place.

discrimination: Unfair treatment based on factors such as a person's race, age, religion, or gender.

Great Depression: A period of economic struggle in the United States and much of the world from 1929 to 1939.

protect: To keep safe.

support: To provide help and guidance.

strike: A stopping of work by employees as a protest against an employer.

FOR MORE INFORMATION

BOOKS

Blas, Terry. *Who Was the Voice of the People? Cesar Chavez.* New York, NY: Penguin Workshop, 2022.

Youssef, Jagger. *The Words of Cesar Chavez.* Buffalo, NY: PowerKids Press, 2023.

WEBSITES

Britannica Kids: Cesar Chavez
kids.britannica.com/kids/article/Cesar-Chavez/352941
Learn more about Cesar Chavez's life and the work that he did.

History for Kids: Cesar Chavez.
www.historyforkids.net/cesar-chavez.html
Find out more about Cesar Chavez.

Publisher's note to educators and parents: Our editors have carefully reviewed these websites to ensure that they are suitable for students. Many websites change frequently, however, and we cannot guarantee that a site's future contents will continue to meet our high standards of quality and educational value. Be advised that students should be closely supervised whenever they access the internet.

INDEX

C
children, 12
Community Service Organization (CSO), 14, 16, 21

F
family, 6, 8
farms, 4, 6, 8, 12
farmworkers, 4, 8, 12, 16, 18, 20

G
grape pickers, 18

M
marriage, 12
Mexican Americans, 4

N
national director, 16

P
pay, 8, 18, 20

R
respect, 14, 18

S
school, 10

U
United Farm Workers of America, 20
U.S. Navy, 10, 12, 21

V
voting, 14